Now and Then

Les Williamson

Poems from the doubtful advantage of an octogenarian

Whitehill Publishing

Published by:
Whitehill Publishing
Just Services
Beaumont Enterprise Centre
72 Boston Road
Beaumont Leys
Leicester LE4 1HB

Tel: 0116 2293102
Fax: 0116 2351844
Email: justandwhitehill@yahoo.com

ISBN: 0-9525838-9-5

Les Williamson has already had considerable success as a novelist, with four novels in print: Jobey (published by Robert Hale - hardback, Methuen - paperback), Bread for All (Robert Hale), Death of a Portrait (Robert Hale) and Crowded Cemetery (Robert Hale). Bread for All and Jobey were both serialised on radio. Les Williamson had assistance in his early writing days from Arts Council England, which helped launch his writing career.

Now and Then is his first full-length poetry collection to be published, although he has long crafted poems and won many prizes for them. Les Williamson shows his extraordinary versatility through this collection. There is no one link drawing them all together, except perhaps the benefit of age and wisdom, from which he demonstrates the whole gamut of human emotions without any hang ups. This collection covers strikes and marches, wars, love and death. He never preaches but has the art of enabling the reader to 'see' the characters portrayed with such clarity as to bring a smile or a tear.

Les Williamson is now eighty three and has been married for sixty three of those years – a marriage he describes lovingly in his poem "Diamond Love". He has achieved much in his life. He served in World War II in Burma, Java and Malaya. He was for several years a tutor of creative writing at Nottingham Prison. He trained as a horticultural judge and judged at many a show over the years, including cakes and flowers when only one judge could be afforded! He holds the Richard Burton Award for Spoken Poetry. He is honorary life president of Eastwood Writers Group. He is great grandfather to twin boys. He has faced heart attacks, cancer, deafness, diabetes and more but, thankfully, lives to tell the tale. He is still "turning out poems on things as they happen" and has plenty more tucked away.

From a life that was relentlessly hard at times, Les Williamson has moved to a time of "sunlight and peace". Whitehill Publishing is honoured to share in his delight at the publication of this insightful collection.

Contents

Contents

Memorial

Straight backs, dark suits and bowler hats
medals here and there
walking sticks and hearing aids
and a chap at the front in a chair.

A closing of ranks, a chumminess
old names recalled as we wait
around the polished memorial
where their memory lies in state.

Old Charlie there, was in the guards
never been long in work
never been the same without the leg
that he left on the beach in Dunkirk.
There's Jonty Brown, lost an eye on the Rhine
(his wife died the following week).

That Mayor ought to have a microphone
or learn how to bloody well speak!

He reads from the 'Roll of Honour'
humanity taking death in its stride
parcelled and labelled in neat chiselled lines
once cheerful chaps with cheerful smiles.

Now as rivers of poppies bleed Autumn to
Winter
let's cherish the names – for THEY have not
died.
JOCK McKAY. TOMMY ATKINS. DAI
DAVIES.
Still strong in our hearts – an invincible tide.

What's in a Name

He was sombre as Abraham Lincoln
chiselled in weathered stone
an Easter Island monolith
inaccessible, standing alone.

He was a man who would stand no nonsense
had stiffened in age and mind
head full of hymns and friends of his youth
upright and downright but kind.

So it wasn't hard to imagine him dead
he'd led such a sober life
he was Byron, gazing on Marathon
a figure of sadness – but still full of fight.

He could smile of course, was always polite
he did as convention decreed
but like the house where he spent his time
a hollowness echoed the deed.

He was more a façade, a reflection
he mirrored whatever you said
which was always correct and carefully weighed
but you never got into his head.

It was as if he had given you notice
that since he had lost his wife
this waxen shell should take his place
as he lived out a ‘sort of’ life.

So it seemed when we stood in the chapel
an unfillable gap in our ranks
that this goodbye to ‘Old Soldier’ Matty
called not just for tears but for thanks.

Pilgrimage

It is sixty years since the flames lit the sky
on the night of a bomber's moon
and the crew played tag with life as the prize –
and death came along (just for the ride).

Then a sound like hail, trashing the trees
shredding the young green leaves
and delicate flesh cringed inside
for the hail was armour piercing.

They buried my friend on a foreign soil
a disciplined death; graves all in a line
there's only been one visit in sixty long years
and shame that I bear, it wasn't mine.

I'm the last one alive who could give him
a name
so the life that he gave hangs just by
this thread
and I'm gorged with guilt, undiluted by time –
for the DEAD cannot grieve for the dead.

But this tenuous thread is a strange device
tugging on memories refusing to die
and the call from such hands, whether dead
or alive

must be answered by and by.

Can I pass my resurrected grief
through a marble slab and the slumbering
years
salving my conscience, making my peace
with a prayer that nobody hears.

Let me go with my frail human spirit
(having no more years in hand)
then try, through friendship or sacred duty
to salvage my soul in that foreign land.

The Silent Road

I still remember brother Jack
across the muddy years
on a primitive farm up a country lane.

We had a language none could share
born of loneliness, despair
no rules, no syntax, nouns or verbs
vibrating air did not make words
to us.
The deaf.

We dug for pignuts when we could beat
the pigs,
which we fed on pea-shells,
having stuffed ourselves with the peas.

We didn't have horns
but (and put it down to the company we kept)
we didn't have words, we had grunts.

Now, eighty years on I hear it again.
Funny that, memories having ears.
So have dreams. About girls,
who don't laugh at you – then walk away
and larks come down to earth to say
'This is our song,

we bring it where we don't belong
to boys who cannot hear.'

A world away from common touch
the suck and throb of waves and such.
The life we knew was 'Nip and Tuck',
one-legged men without a crutch.

One day they took my Jack away
(the flickering candle keeping dark at bay)
left me to a lonely world
as the shortness of his life unfurled.
But I recall the better things
when Jack and I on silent wings
saw the egg of every bird
and nothing of the world was heard.

What joy we had.
What love we shared.

Dream Time

Rooted deep in my childhood dreams
is a village I called my own
where sticklebacks gleamed in friendly
streams
and fourteen pounds weighed a stone
and, would you believe, no mobile phone.

Morning mushrooms in the grass
apple pie and rabbit stew
sunshine pulling at my sleeve
birdsong hung on morning dew.

Farmers produce at the church
scrubbed and clean at the vicar's feet
a 'Fire-escape' from a very real hell
saving their souls with barley and wheat.

And daily the gobbling geese were seen
While magpies sparred with the vicarage
crows
and ducks on the pond were part of the scene
and the poacher's pocket was still in vogue.

And yes, there was honey still for tea
if you knew where to go and who to see
and the plod-foot cows knew their way
back home

and Grandad’s name was chiselled in stone
on the cenotaph at the village green.

These are dreams of a place that didn’t survive
oooh – but wasn’t it good just being alive.

Grandma and 'The Pit'

I remember an old rocking chair
and an ample, kindly Grandma.
Grandma's house was to do with potatoes
and cabbage
lip-smacking dinners and thick black gravy.

My uncles came home in their 'pit-dirt'
silent and unwashed until they had eaten.
They were macho, liniment smelling and hairy
full of testosterone and prejudice,
but enough, we're talking Grandma's here.
Flat cap squarely on her head, built like a
Roman wall
she could lean over a ponch-tub and make the
pit shirts fly.
She poured iodine into our open wounds
which felt like acid
get a ball back from a neighbour with a single
fixed stare,
'lay out' a body for a funeral and put on a ham
and tongue tea.
(Bodies were always kept in the parlour in
those days).

She woke at five-fifteen every morning
without any aid from alarm clocks.

By five thirty the table was full of bread and
dripping
and bottles of cold tea.

She knew the price of bacon in every shop.
Bacon, apparently, being the yardstick for
value.
She could peg a rug in a week. And –
sharp-eared as any dog she could pick out the
iron-shod feet
of her menfolk from half a street away
then have the inevitable rice pudding on
the table
when they set foot through the door.
The measure of a good wife and mother was
to be putting
out the dinner as her men entered the door.
The skin on the pudding was black as your hat
and thicker than a bull's ear.
It was pudding first in those days. Meat later.
With luck.

Roaring fires, plenty of discipline
local accent thick as treacle.
Co-op 'divi'. Cobbling shoes. Cake in the
pantry.
Not a lot to write home about, really.
It must have been Grandma herself, then.

She’s still around here, somewhere.
Poking the fire. Spreading washing on the
range …

A Collection for Grandad

There are times when the ghost of the coal
comes stealing along in the night
and takes me back to my childhood days
to the families who fought the good fight.

Grandma sat by the side of the road
it was Friday night and the men had been paid
she had Grandad's cap placed square on
her knees
for a miner's cap was the sign of his trade.

Pitmen never showed much emotion
they were 'strong' and all it implied
but they knew Grandad was in his best
nightshirt
with pennies on each of his eyes.

To 'collect' was a mining tradition
whenever a breadwinner died
now the streets are heavy with Grandad's
ghost
chilling the night like a rising tide.

Grandad was small through living on tripe
and was blamed on all sides for their plight
but I knew this lean old wolf of a man

as a giant in body and mind.

And when I'd done wrong, was afraid of
some fist
I'd rush to his sheltering side
and many's the blow he's taken for me
as I buried my head in his thighs.

On a Friday, there'd be a rice pudding
then he'd slice off the top with his knife
and giving a grin he'd 'slive' it to me
glancing over his shoulder in case we
were spied.

They took me to see him up creaking old stairs
all dark and forbidding with death in the room
he was cold as I touched the blue-scarred
hands
just a lump in a bed on a cold afternoon.

They gave me a slap for holding his hand
which had held me so tight to his knee
and the memory comes strong through the
years between
there was nobody crying but me.

The Hard Men. 1926
(Year of the General Strike)

The fields of my youth were thorn and rock
yielding nothing but places to hide,
a retreat where we met like a squabble
of crows
so close to the earth we could hear its cries.

And sometimes when summer was calling
strong
we'd abandon school and fly to the fields
our traditional home which laid no blame
we were one with the magpie and fox.

In the '26 strike the colliers came
digging surface coal (compacted mud)
thrusting upwards, showing its hem
to horny hands, tempting them on.

The coalfield now was a battlefield
our fathers fighting with picks
gobbing coal-black phlegm, dark as the pit –
full stops into civilised discourse.

They raped our field which was foreign to them
as the coal dust mascara'd their eyes
gulping scalding tea, 'mashed' in the field

leaving pig-pink lips where the dust had been.

I returned to the field from a distant land
to a moonscape of hollows and holes
seeing long dead miners on silenced air
a vision of time gone by.

Small men, caps down hard. Sawdust floors in
the pub.
Dogs and kids, flogged into silence
waiting to take the 'mester' home.
The bare-fist fighter. Every village had one.

And we were just waiting our turn
when somewhere along the way ...
civilisation happened.

The Pits

Grandad insists he was a number once
as he returns from dreams of world war two.

'My army number is branded into my brain
Six wasted years it says. 1940 to 1946.
And good years they were
not like the tatty things we get now.'
He has the winter smell of all ex-miners,
woolly and minty. Not used to the cold.

'Afore that we had a good pit – not many
getting killed.
Six years though. Six must be an unlucky
number.'
'Six? Why six?'
'Six months. That's what they've give me.
Mebbe more if that stuff clears my lungs a bit.
My old army number's turned up trumps,
though.
I've made it me pin.
No! Got to stop saying that. Secret.
I shall say it to Saint Peter, though.
Proudly. And afore long.'

Grandad settles into his easy chair
his medals in a drawer. His memories bright
as a new pin.

Some of them.

Taking death in his stride
while Autumn bleeds into Winter
on this now sleeping coalfield ..
        of dreadful dreams.

The Face of War

Christmas oozed from the well-bred shops
warm with the scent of money
but it never quite reached the pavement
and the pile of old clothes that was Ernie,
a mouth organ wedged where his teeth
should be.

A box on the floor held his meagre 'take',
some very small change and a broken
mince pie
Some lads had thrown the crumpled pie
and were crowding now with menacing sounds
listening and laughing at 'Lili Marlene'
from this ragged old man, who had dropped
from a star.

The old chap turned to face them, dropping
his scarf
from the stricken mess that had once been
a face.
There were shrieks and cries from the
young ones
who scattered as if from a bomb.

And his mind flashed back to a far-Eastern
shore

where a shell-burst blossomed in orange
                                        and flame.
In England then, it was Summer
and the hawthorns bloomed down every lane.

But the shells were a thousand stabs of light
the smell of roast flesh and animal fright
where coffins were things that were yours
                                        for keeps
and you travelled alone down one-way streets.

It was sixty years since he'd left the fray
hate and malice now burned away
with a few more empty years to be filled
in a silence only death can build.

For fate had dealt him a losing hand
hunting for gold in a barren land
with a face that had long since blown away
so his fighting words had feet of clay.

Yes I Remember Christmas

It was dark and chill in the quiet streets
which clung to the edge of the mine
and the boy had been told there was
magic about
with the stars all turned up extra bright.

Could the magic be church bells keening
their sound
on the cutting edge of a slim new moon
or the wind-splintered snow round the old
street lamp
playing its arctic tune.

He stayed for a while in an entry
felt for the heat from the stone
that backed on a fire which burned within
he was seven and all alone.

But carol singing had driven him out
while folks seemed to have money to burn
the paper round was a steady job
but this was a real chance to earn
but I'll tell you the way I collected my pay.

There were pennies still hot from the top of
a stove

there were some in a chamber pot
there were dogs which held you fast by
the arm
while the owners took whatever you'd got.

It was all a good laugh if you didn't freeze
while they played such grown-up tricks
but money didn't grow on trees
not in nineteen hundred and twenty six.

Words

The consultant speaks.
'Put your clothes on
we'll have a little chat.'

A little chat!
I laugh. An explosion of relief.
Such harmless words, nothing dreadful
or terminal.

I dress eagerly,
almost wink at this 'God-man'
a smile on my face.
But he looks at me sadly
searching for words –
which will never be 'chat'.

The moment freezes.
Escape! But where to hide from his words.
My mind is a blank.

Then I see through his window a single
daffodil.

Tenacious.
Nodding to me. A symbol of Spring
and the frailty of life
but I still fear the unspoken words.

He uses his words now.
But. They are not reaching. Not up to the job.
They fall at my feet, rejected.
Good old ears, that's what friends are for.
I hide behind my ears
but reality insists, incisive as a scalpel
scraping away at the nerve.

Someone is holding my hand
as I hammer at my disbelief.

        Stop all the clocks.

Prologue
Enter left. Old man with a stick.

Time owes us nothing.
We invented it, a yardstick for our own backs.
Mute commentator, disparagingly honest
it condemns with the silent evidence of the
status quo.
Nothing falls through its net.
Invisible, untouchable, yet mutilates all things.
Genghis Khan was an angel.
Fact.

I had a birthday yesterday,
eighty-two.
Not one card through the post.

Abandon hope all ye who enter here,
the arena of old age.
Politeness, condescension, air kissing,
prissy smiles.

Sod the postman ..
and all who live by his false values.

He's nothing but a lifeline. An umbilical cord.
At 82. Who needs him?

Well I bloody do.

I do. I do. I do.

No Hiding Place

My grandson was two as he faced his mum,
she was holding a small blue car,
both of them knew that the car wasn't his.

'So where did this come from George?'
She smiled as she teased him on.

A young friend's party, the day before
was the probable scene of his crime
seeing the end of his innocent years.
He'd fallen a prey to vice!

What awful emotions the question stirred
as the silence tortured his mind
so much so that my heart gave him words
leaving my honour and ethics behind.

I dropped to my knees with smothering love
preparing to lie – to perjure – contrive
offering words from my devious soul
inured in the crucibled patchwork of life.

For soon enough must decisions be made
which require a wise head for a guide
and two small years isn't time enough
to surround oneself with places to hide.

Diamond Love. 60 Years.

We loved from where we were
not from candle-light and pink champagne.
You said I had the voice of a tree
full of timbre
and I recall when your breath in my chest
set the adrenaline running like liquid fire.
We had a war that went on forever.
Both afraid of the war-torn clouds of ’42.
But we had our words. Such words
as were never born of thoughts
but somehow had always been there to
cling to.
Can’t remember what they were just now!

Volcanic love, hardening through the pitiless
years
of make do and mend.
Memories of passion, love against a farmyard
gate –
now closed.

Has it really been sixty years?

Aye, and lonely jungle nights with only
Ivor Novello’s ‘Lilacs in the Spring’ for
company.

Then home at last, the thrill of hanging up
her coat
and quietly hugging the sumptuous ghost
which still clung snug and warm inside.
So real. So near. And hugging back!
Arms, longing enough to defy common sense.
It's what separates us from the apes.
The touch-paper of real emotions.

Breathe in, the years of longing
gathered now in her hair and her neck.
The magic of man and woman
clasped there in unashamed wanting.
Just asking to love – and be loved.
And then to be quietly together in the twilight.

Aunt Maud

She had always been there, Aunt Maud,
lips primly pursed, for a kiss.
Part mother, part port in a storm.
Indispensable cog in the daily grind
a turn of the wheel on a quiet day
making no trouble.
A clock on the wall, convenient.
No 'Please.' No 'Thanks'. No need.
She was just Maud. With a smile on her face
and a thousand ways
of pushing her love into needful places.

Till the day came along when SHE needed
love,
for herself.
She needed 'Care'.
A four letter word.
Disguised as 'Cherish'. 'Treasure'. Etc ..
See any thesaurus.
A 'Paper Paradise' is 'Care'.

Each day left its mark
an obscene scar on the soul of Maud.
Laugh lines. Laugh long gone.
Days heavy with time.
Settling in. Slow as November pears.

Empty years. Brittle diction. Lowered lids.
Whiskered chin. Death row in pretty chintz
until the welcome day – she saw – and was
                                                                not afraid.

And now, my memory. Strewn with guilt.
Aunt Maud. Who made no trouble.
And a love that still pushes.
        Where it hurts.

As Time Goes By

'Tell me Grandpa, what is it like to be old?'
(A five year old to an eighty three).

Your whole life in a nutshell, then.

Wouldn't like to do it all again.
(That sort of cuts it down to size).

There was dodging bombs during the war.
Winnie's blood sweat and tears.
Him and his carrot and turnip pie!
Moonlight Serenade, though, cuddled up with -
No. Got to be more to it than that.
There were hunger marches.
'In Africa? No! In this country.'

Then there was the start of television.
'Eh? A time before TV?'
Yeah, of course. (Just us and the dinosaurs).

Finished school at thirteen.
Apprenticed for seven lean years
to pale lean men ... forgotten how to smile.
Awaiting our turn to be pale and lean.
There was the battle of Britain.
The atom bomb.

What's it like to be old?
I trace the stucco of my face with bony fingers
reading the Braille of memories there
tightly corseted – in the ways of yesterday
living etched into my face as year piles upon
year.

Cold as a worm in Winter
the survival prospects of a hairy hedgehog.

That's what it's like to be old.
In a nutshell.

Not of this Earth

In the restaurant she presented me with the bill
and an obviously pleasant remark.

'Sorry dear.' I replied. 'Deaf.'
Pointing to my ears and smiling broadly
in an effort to separate myself from
Quasimodo.
She stared back,
Surprise, puzzlement, embarrassment
chasing across her features
fighting her built-in happy face
that went with the job.

She spoke again.
I shook my head, pointing to my ears.
She glanced at an assistant
who had frozen in mid-something or other,
her corner eye taking me in.

Poor devil. Out on his own.
I was on the wrong side of a great divide,
a subject for later discussion.
The deaf man.

I took the change, tipped more than necessary
and legged it into the great outdoors.

She had been young, impossibly slim
and as accommodating as could be expected
on first encountering an alien species.

Funeral at Christmas

Christmas Eve morning,
in church waiting for the coffin.

Sonorous moan from the organ
anaesthesia for the soul.
And along the walls,
Brass plaques, frayed flags and other
bric-a-brac.

Can we bury this collision of emotions
behind the brash goodwill of Christmas.

Now the coffin arrives
at odds with the glistening tree
which is winking, beckoning, seducing.

Christ's birthday
but the shallow shine of floss and fairy lights
adds polish to the coffin.
The here and now
where a true and wonderful friendship
is contained at the last, within this box.
Just the residue. A carcass.
A many medalled chest
reduced now to fragile memory.
A grandchild has laid a cracker on the coffin

and inside?
A paper hat? Or … a heart ripping week ..

Lives, tethered by shadows –
and the tree twinkles on
with its message of birth and death –
and the brief ‘in between’.

Deep down where we are so terribly alone.

The Game of Life

The dice for the game were missing
and five-year George was waiting to throw
then a smile of triumph came over his face
'We can play without dice, you know.'

'Watch me Grandpa, I'm throwing for you.'
Then he rolled the invisible dice
as his eyes went chasing over the board ..
'You've only got two, that's not very nice.'

Then he threw for himself and gave me a look
too young to contain any tricks,
'Well just look at that, it's my lucky day
you can't see but I've thrown double six.'

I looked at the shining innocent eyes
unburdened as yet with the ways of the world
naïve to the 'Getting your nose in front'
as the pattern of life began to unfurl.

There's a force that drives the seminal sperm
and fills our lives with haste
that is showing our way to the distant stars
with never a second to waste.

For man, so fragile in body and mind

knows the clock of the cosmos remorselessly
ticks
where dice are thrown by an unknown hand
and can deal sudden death or a six.

Hospital Visit

He stares at the wall, despite my approach.
I give him the big smile,
my own flesh and blood – the rest – a vacuum.
Tied to me by a cord,
a thread that will not break,
only strangle.

Where tenderness should be
there's a stare of vacant menace.
My loving greetings fall at his feet,
a jackpot of memories cascading to the floor.

His eyes, mirror-shallow
look out but do not see
and I am holding hands with heartache.
It is a pilgrimage to a shrine
bearing gifts from a shriven heart
hardening unpityingly to indifference
as the disease takes its pound of flesh.
An infectious numbness prevails.
His every face a mask
from his dreadful box of tricks.

Labels on clothes, labels on shoes …
and people.
'Sing-along-a-Max' in the background.

‘You need Hands’ … to change a catheter
give a pat on the head (that was once so wise)
pull slippers over a heel
wipe a chin or a plastic geranium.

Waves of heat, pressing down on a cardigan
sea.
The Doldrums. Here be dragons.
But what is love
that asks for nothing in return –
a cliché.

But I do need something in return.
I do. I do. I do.

The Quick and the Deaf

In church I sat when the others sat
stood when the others stood
and there must have been music somewhere
for the congregation knew when to sing.
(You can't read the lips of an organ).

I looked at the coffin, bright in the Easter sun
as the light poured in through an open door
revealing daffodils
swaying their trumpets in harmony having
served their time in the tomb.
The trees, more reluctant, feigned death,
their time had not yet come.
I glanced through the door for something to do,
time goes more slowly when you are deaf.

Cows were outside, looking at me,
listening to the prayers.
The one in front lowered its head
as in worship.
The others followed its lead
nervous, unsure.
Another gathering for group-comfort.
Two congregations, afraid of the other side.
A moment of closeness
an almost touching of species.

Then, with a reassurance that life goes on
it was heads down again,
into the sand.
How the brain does ramble at times like this.

Then someone shut the door –
and we returned to the ultimate silence –
from which we all came,
some of us, able to tell the difference.

Me, Myself and I

I'm the one who is faking an interest
accustomed to being alone,
alone in a crowded room, that is,
where I live in a world of my own.

Somebody laughs and it brings me back
from a world which I share with none
I give them a smile and a knowing look
but the words that were spoken are gone.

I'm the one looking round 'til I see moving lips
then I know that the sound comes from 'there'
while puckering browed, I study the silence
my grapple on life is a stare.

I mouth the mundane passwords
to friends along the way –
comfort words – the cry of birds -
pasting a smile on the face of the day.

I quarter your face like a hawk on the make
while remembering a long-distant thrush
lost in the too-long twilight of life
which is becoming a permanent hush.

Tedium drags at the daily clock

pulling the hours into days.
Ears? They're for anchoring spectacles
or for holding your hat off your face.

But I keep in touch with eyes and smiles
and feelings which still have a heart
and a touch of the hand if it comes my way
Pagliacci – just playing his part.

Gone Beyond

I wandered into the graveyard,
the old part – where nobody goes
and stood amongst the beech trees,
over-bearing towers of doom.

Not a smile between them.
No 'Wrinkled Old Bark' beloved of poets.
The soil, surrounded by sombre centuries
may support an odd crocus
perhaps even a rose, windblown, hanging
its head.
The gravestones hoard silence and time
clasped in their hard marble arms.

All that is human, with warmth and light
now wrung from the weeping air.
The place casts a spell on itself,
soaked in its sepia years.
This grave, at the end of the world.

Why am I here?
Where silence rules – declares its presence.
There is no sky here
just a 'grim reaping' of people long gone.
I am gooseflesh. Henflesh. Shivering skin
soaking in tears.

Let me grieve.
I'll lift up my head.
Tomorrow? Well, sometime.

The Lakes

Sudden breeze on the water
bringing a chill
goose-pimpling the surface of the lake.

Willow branches paint wavy shadows
where the pike lies, one eye ever open
watching the boats dressed overall
in fine Summer cottons
clinging now to lithe young bodies.

High in the hills the rowan roots cling
to the lichened stone
where the wind is keening its knives
on the permanent ice.
Awaiting its chance to remind you
that the snug intimacy of June umbrellas
the soft warm breath of man and woman
are just for the moment,
transient as the swallow
fondling the morning air through his tail.
The mood of the day so perfect
I recall in soft focus
a day of deep memories
having no voice
but growing more eloquent with the years.

Not for Sale

Just a rack of men's coats in a charity shop
a mosaic of life and death,
these nowhere – nobody spaces
that – strung together – become slices of life.

But it isn't just wear that has formed the
contours,
fashioned the shape of the ghost in each coat
it is hugging and tugging from tiny hands
long woven into fabric
where some of the ghosts still cling.

Immaculate blazers, ram-rod straight,
they hang in a sober row
empty sleeves that no longer beckon
to the sanctuary of 'Dad'.

We move down the rail quite unaware
how long each coat has been empty.
Do the family peep in now and again,
touch the thing that they hold so dear
trailing its memories through yesterday's dust
to a place where things must be priced –
that have no price.

Abandoned now for intrusive presence

like the undertow of a deep silent tide.
The nameless coats, the colonel and the
corporal's
in a charity shop. The ultimate leveller.

Memories still tethered.
And they're not for sale. Not at any price.

Church Flower Festival Today

From the sanctified air of the church
thick with the inertia of years
comes stiff-necked music from the organ
floating past brass plaques
'Sacred to the memory' of bygone bigwigs
looking down solemn noses at young and
tattooed flesh
leggy and loud with youth.

But here come the flowers
rampant with the smell of lilies,
sermons and sucked mints.

Cottage pinks by the tiny fistful
crammed in slits and crannies
children's posies, quaking grass
wild flowers reeds and weeds, common
meadow flowers
now happy prisoners of the church
and proud for once, to be on the front row.

Poppy heads are pearls
seeds are precious stones
palms are fans from ancient Rome.
Gargoyles and driftwood dragons
become things of exotic beauty.

Laughing scampering children,
gossiping sober adults, blood bonding.
A ready smile for everyone – including
strangers.
The church, giving out life by the handful
shining like a bar of new soap
scrubbing doubt from every nook and cranny
of the mind.

The Flower Festival.
Brings freshness amongst the dust.
And religion – from the knees into the heart.

Christmas

It's here and it's lovely.
A brittle silence holds the air
children – shining eyes aglow
have time for once to stop and stare.

You've sent those cards with love and kisses
everyone with 'All good wishes'
lighting the dark of deep December.
Mistletoe and Uncle Joe –
last year – remember?

Bright shops and music in the snow
reindeer bells and HO HO HO.
Old folks with soapy polished skin
memories frail but joining in
grasping for names – 'That's Mary's son?'
'You don't mean Jesus!'
'Shut up, Mum.'

How brief the peace that fills the air
that lifts its head as if in prayer
but time slips by, it's dark already.
'Sherry trifle! Take it steady.'

Spangled seconds sparkle by
out there the world is in full cry

but here, it's love and soft warm skin
so put your arms round kith and kin.
Feet up! Drink up! Whinge who may
shout 'Joy for us.'

'It's Christmas Day.'

The Stately Homes of England

No dogs, ice cream or Stanley knives.

We edge respectfully through the library doors,
floor carpeted in heavy silence.
No hilarity in here,
let it brood in the gloom of its own making,
its atmosphere of solemn authority
laid out in rows of black judicial facts.
Full of old ghosts – from Homer to Donne.

Through an open window, Summer takes
a sniff
at the furniture polished dark.
Outside the wind makes a 'Mexican Wave'
in the Wisteria blossom
but the timeless petrified trunk
puts a stop to such frivolous antics.

No chandeliers, cut glass or mirrors here
the books have turned their backs on
the world
like the retinue of the ancient pharaohs
incarcerated with their masters.

Here is an awesome essence of knowledge
coagulating into viscous pools.

Dusty memories, quiet ordered years.
Wisdom wrung from silence and solitude.
Tread softly for these are the great men
frozen for the long journey through time.

Trees in Winter

There's a ring of frosted trees
surrounding a frozen pond
implacable, sapless, out of time
held in thrall to Winter's wand.

Needle-rich pines in shining white
deep in hibernation
delicate birch in silvered snow
in midnight desolation.

But the wrinkled bark has a chilly smile
at the seagulls starving cry
knowing deep within the wood
the time to live and the time to die.

For the trees have sent their leaf-green
dreams
to join the daffodils
to listen for the coming spring
and wake before the blackbird sings.

Poetry is

Poetry is
a journey into the farthest reaches of the mind.
A searching for the words
to be distilled
having smoothed off all the edges.
When you grovel to the brain
for a word that is almost there.
A hovering on the edge of consciousness
in a place that is always Spring.
A place where words look at you and smile
knowing they are just right.
And you smile back.

Where bats swing to and fro on the shadows
and a thrush throws sound at the morning.
But you are here for the words
and if they come right – do not disturb.
They are bricks in a wall that will endure.
Deep poetry is part mystery
for such moments are only lent,
they are never given.

They are stored away in a magic place, to
mature –
to use … when they are good and ready.

Song of the Flowers

The florists shop, our enchanted home.
An equal embrace for weddings or funerals.
We switch roles at the drop of a coin,
society's maids of all work.
Wreaths on one side, bridal bouquets on the
other
from buckets to bouquets in one pragmatic
leap
which way shall we turn for our shilling today.

We are the acceptable face of grief
closer than flesh without the embarrassment.
Halfway to heaven,
the only visible link that males are allowed.
Stepping stones
bonding what is to what has been
milking each moment.
I loved. You loved. We loved
in a thousand tongues
without sound.

We say what was left unsaid
are thrown by the bride, clutched by the dead.
We are the flowers.
Won't you buy the pretty flowers.

Room With a View

They're giving the city a new silhouette,
the line is being improved
an industrial revolution
from the worst of times to the best of times.

There's never been such a smashing time
since the days of old King Ludd
when fires were set and deeds were done
in the name of the common good.

But now the dark satanic mills
are crumbling to the juggernauts
for high rise flats and parks for cars,
'carbuncles' … 'sores and warts'.

But here and there an empty shell
still marks our heritage
cheek by jowl with glass and chrome
and the champagne style of expense
accounts.

From here we can look out into the dark
to where an old factory still patterns the stars
marking the place where children worked
manufacturing money and terrible scars.

It's just an old workplace, no feelings or
ghosts.

That's a reasonable, logical thought
but the shadow is gorged with the weight of
guilt

of this terrible school where heartache was
taught

and the shadow it casts is a long black pall
which hangs over tables .. carnations .. and all.

Bon Appetit!

Painting Lesson

What a wonderful world is coming our way
we've broken the code or our own DNA.
We've climbed into bed with the
world-wide-web
transplanted our kidneys, doctored our eggs
cosied up warm to the greenhouse effects
embraced new computers, reproduced without
sex.
Diverted rogue comets with lasers and such
we are Lords of all we survey.

We are painting the picture to suit our own
plan
while polluting the planet as fast as we can.
There's red on the canvas – that looks like
blood -
what next?
Well there's holes in the ozone, germs we
can't kill
'laptops' defy us, they won't stand still
re-inventing their part in the plot.
They strive to achieve impossible dreams
like emotion, awareness and love.

But the difficult bit is colouring men
if you mix up their colours the harmony's gone

the brighter the white, the darker the night
should we colour by numbers, let God be our
guide
would He lead us to Eden in the fullness of
time?

But what of this God who stands alone
whose image is sacred in gold or in stone?
Was creation caused at his gentle call –
the ocean's roar or the wild star's fall.
Did He give the tree its friendly grin
that draws both hawk and sparrow in?
Can He feel in the shade, the bramble barbs
sharp as a wildcat's claws
see the fox's smile as he sees his kill
through Summer's open doors.

For the world is nobody's oyster
we make of it what we can
and the bountiful crop of the Summer
may be nothing but chaff for the Winter's fan.

Chesil Beach

A stony beach where rolling rocks
are turned by timeless tides
smoothed and polished, stealing colour
from wind-washed waves and the sky.

Swirling and surging the waters push
like an egg-bound turtle reaching her shore
and the hollow sound as the stones click-clack
was a wake up call for dinosaurs.

Abandoned and barren the eggs of stone,
spawn of the sun and the sea
acquire the tactile cultured feel
of a diamond dusted Fabergé.

These precious stones have lain in peace
buffed by the sand since before life began
shuffled and shaped by a watery hand …
treasure laid down for the joy of man.

We choose from earth's great bounty
just what to call our own
jewels rare beyond compare
or a 'Time-Made' heap
of lovable stone.

Where time is compressed to be held in the
hand
written in stone – the facts of the past
but the future still hangs by a tender thread
to be told by the runes …
which are still to be cast.

That's Life

1.30 pm and the door thuds shut behind me.
Steel on steel.
It will open again about four – tea time –
when the writers' class is finished
and badly bruised egos have been salved a
little –
when I have teased something good out of
their work.

But I am here to teach, not spread healing
balm
though old enough to have made a few
mistakes myself.
A human amongst humans.
We are a snapshot of life from the great
unknown
to which we return – and no-one to hold our
hand.

I look at the class, the good the bad and the
ugly.
A handful of men from any high street.
No horns. No built-in typecasting as villains
just a group .. in need of rehabilitation.
One, in need of more than that, a born killer.
Sitting on his own, an empty smile.

He is called Sam. A caged bird even in
present company.
I think of the poem he turned out last week
sort of scarred into my brain.

Life As We Know It

I listen as life beats a path to my door
with more empty years in hand.
These I shall share with my paper
and words: which are sometimes so right
they look at me and smile.
And I smile back, knowing how they feel.

Words stand in for friends.
others are more deep and intimate
soft, warm and smooth.
I cup them in my hands
but in the deep of the night
they become … shallow things.

Sam

When the key turns in the lock
we go our separate ways.
Me to the world at large
him to the splendour of his dreadful cell.
To dream his impossible dreams.

Life

We do not have horns
just wives and children
(and the libido of once dominant males).
But I face each day
in the custodial world that is known as 'CAT A'.
High Security. Watch the bastard.
Spit in his dinner –
if you like. It's up to you.

I sit at the back of the writers' class
pondering my record which states.
'Has killed with his hands and could do so
again.'
My brain is a fog of confusion and hate.

My heart is seared to a steel-barred square,
a patch of blue from the outside world
and it draws like a racing tide.
A shopping mall. People.
Making plans. A woman!

While the teacher, taking this world for
granted,
passes a couple of sweets.
Buy them from any shop you happen to be
passing.

(If you belong to this world).
They lie in my hand,
the hand that would reach for the sky –
but must pull down my dreams,
while my head, full of words
spills only bile on to paper.

Words. They pound in my ears
a roaring ocean of hate.
I'm the man at the back
looking at 'Life'. (That's twelve years. Plus?)
One long black night
folding black upon pitiless black.
'Life?'

Try 'Death'.
        Now you have it.

A Ghost in the Cotswolds

The Poetry Book of Golden Moments
25 Pence.

From the bargain pile in a charity shop.
Price scribbled by busy staff
but inside the front cover –
in a laboured hand.

'I pass on this book for you to enjoy'
Rosie.

A heart given free with a book.
I could almost smell the cider.

Impossible now to discard this book,
this comfort toy in time-polished black
which the anonymous Rosie needed to share.
The simple joy of familiar things,
this homely treasure of rhythm and rhyme
from a pleasantly cluttered attic
where the clock has chimed away
the unbroken hours of nothing to say.

A gentle goodbye and good luck
to whoever should find these words.
A leaving of something behind –

a signpost for living.
Building bridges with only a smile
and a tatty book.
At twenty five pence –
an unrepeatable offer.

From Rosie.

A Love for all Seasons

Sea-side out of season, chill, impersonal.
Scarves and woolly hats
lost in the misty greyness
of sea and far-off ships.
While near at hand, distant people.
Flotsam on the Winter tide.
An iceberg of inertia
cold in the loveless air.

And the dark, somehow impatient
and not waiting for the night
hovers over the cliffs,
the out-of-season cliffs.

While in a café, perched on a rock,
(all steam and casual staff),
a desultory air. Time killing stares.
Blank eyes over tea and coffee.

And yet –
at a side table
and just for today,
an almost touching of two lives.
As unforgivable as ships too close in the night.
Hands now inches apart. Millions of inches.

Memories of things which never took place.
Treasure. To bury in the sands of time.

No map. No X to mark the precious spot
except a lasting kiss from hand to hand
and a love as strong as any tide.

An Innocent in Venice

He was selling bits of Italy
in St Mark's square.

Loud, aggressive,
adorned with his souvenirs.
Quick with the lingo, quicker still with the lira.
He sensed my puzzled stare
as he thrust a handful of short-change
into my tourist palm.

He pressed on with his spiel,
kept going with the hard sell
spreading himself before the crowd
and I was history.
He had moved on
without a backward glance.

I applauded him … with my silence.
His patter was a barrage at which I baulked.
Me. So touchy in my moral values.

He had worked on his image like a
Michelangelo.
Intrinsic to the Venetian cut and thrust
as the gondolas.
This rogue was a maestro on his own rostrum.

The music of the Mafia flowed from his fingers
and I was entranced.
Could I pull down his house of cards
for petty change,
this consummate worker of the crowds.

I became one more sucker in Venice
unable to desecrate such a work of art.

Or was it sheer cowardice
that made me walk away?

Farmer's Wife
(Defeats Herd of Cows)

She took his hand firmly and held on.
Despite thirty years of marriage she felt his
reluctance.
At home, she knew he would pull away,
a stile to mend, a barn to be shored,
cows to be milked.
Clara, Daisy, Buttercup, he spoke to them all
as they scent-marked the very air,
the great plod-foot hairy beasts.
Well, they were a hundred miles away now.
She had this perfect day between sea and
heather,
a day off from bovine gravitas.
For breathing in sunshine.
For Dr Johnson's favourite pastime –
'Stuffing and staring'.
Bathing all the penniless places in gold
hugging the air, floating in blue.
'Admiring' the huge expanse of ocean
which terrified her,
licking its lips – waiting its chance.

She put her arms around his neck
and her whole self into a gentle rendering of
'People will say we're in love.'

She moved her hips.
This was not dancing, it was snogging to music
cheek to cheek and getting closer.
'Happy, darling?'
He nodded, tears forming as he spoke.
'No fool like an old fool, Eh?' He whispered.
He looked, really looked, into the brown of her
eyes.
She spread her fingers and fondled his hair,
drew him to her on this perfect day.

She had put those cows in their place,
good and proper.

Maisie one. Cows nil.

Nightmare

In the never-ending dead-night of the ward,
a panic button .. and a rushing of feet.
Two slim nurses take the weight,
literally.
I crane my neck from a few beds away
to where Sam is suspended
in their practised grip.
They have one eye on the monitor.

In a small island of light
hands move swiftly.
A strange intimacy,
the miracle of human concern,
life reaching to life.
A gentle nurse-thing. Not taught.
No curriculum could encompass.

The old man fights for his life
while a touch of more than hands
responds.
On the monitor, a hesitant blip
becomes a steady stream
until, in the crucible of high drama –
a patting back into the pillows
of a face that is bone on bone
but a heart that is still beating.

Still joined to the young
in thankfulness.
For, as Sam would put it –
‘A few more empty days.’
To tell us ‘What good years the Lord used to
send.
Not at all like the tatty things we get now!’

All in a night’s work.

Alf

Cloud Nine
Somewhere in
England

In a rural country market place
in a time-forgotten town
there's a seventy year old Angel
careering up and down
helmet covered in slogans
'I've been everywhere.'
His super-charged velocipede –
a battery-driven chair.

Laughing eager youngsters
squeeze between his knees
while back at his base more toddlers wait
by the stall that sells hot peas.

His face is creased with speckled smiles,
a halo of skin and whiskers
roly-poly cuddly clown
feet fixed firmly but not on the ground
as he swings along his yellow brick road
priorities settled and sorted.

No votes to be found – it's purely for fun
but you have to belong to a huggy young club.

Feel the love that surrounds each homely stall
from that happy old bean-bag – sat on by all.

Traffic wardens and council officials beware
Alf has the Angels on his side …
                    The real ones.

Where There's a 'Will'

Mabel didn't hear the world go by these days
everyone whispering and tip-toeing about
and hearing aids not worth a toss.
But the rings she had just taken off –
they had a satisfying sound,
whirring and chinking in the china jewellery
tray.

Gold!
Amazing how THAT made itself heard.
There was something about it that by-passed
the ears.
It spoke to relations living miles away,
even young people .. never willing to sit at her
feet
Old Mabel knew how to bring them to heel.

Gold was a treasure you didn't hide.
The trick was to put it in the shop window.
A cheap trick
but there were times when she had not had a
visit for weeks.
That was when she scattered the gold about,
coffee table gold.

She cackled.
The Pied Piper was just an amateur.

Memorial (2)

Johnson asked me round again today,
for coffee
and 'incidentally' to see his sweet peas.
He still grows them.
Says memories are more precious than
money.

Mine have got virus, he says.
Knows everything.
He can see them from behind his 'gazebo'.
Gazebo! 'Sound of Music'. Romantic
interludes ...
he's living in a fantasy world.

He has to stand on two bricks to see me.
I can see him, too, from a certain position –
he's not got all the bricks.

He's a muck and mystery man.
'It's all in the stars'.
Well not all, or he wouldn't have been caught
out.
It hit him for six!

Sow when the moon is on the wane. Or wax.
Or something.
Dip the seeds in paraffin,

keep the mice (and the devil) away.
He puts tins of water under his beans
swears they will put on an extra inch
trying to reach the water.
'Beans with brains'.

Anyway he doesn't grow them now.
SHE was the one for the beans.

His rhubarb's gone to seed. Not noticed it yet.
There's worse things than having virus in
your peas.
He waits for me going into the garden
then he pounces – with his whisper-thin voice.
'Let me show you this. Come and look at that.
Have another cup of tea. Too nice to go in just
yet.'
I've been given the grand tour six times
already.

You should just hear him.
On about the lingering fragrance of shared
sweet peas
and … would you believe …
the sweet pain of nostalgia!

What ails the bloody man.
She's gone.

Harry

He's not really dead.
Not Harry.
Not the type.
Don't ask me why.
I have only words - to present my case
and they only deal in black and white ..
Hello and goodbye. Dead or alive.
Such shallow things.

It's not that I can't let go.
We were never that close,
he was just part of the things that were.
He belonged to the status quo
like Monday follows Sunday,
a man to rely on –
to be there.

Harry.

You were made of sterner stuff
having no truck
with that sort of muck …
six feet underground
like some common man
on the omnibus.
Not at all one of us.

No. He's not really dead, isn't Harry,
beyond sight, sound and smell
not your common or garden dead.
Not Harry.
You were no life and soul
but a corner stone
that fastened all life together.

You were Harry.

The End of the Line

Old Jonty was always a railway man
headful of steam for forty years
a man who was kept on the temperate rails
by the sobering sight of shining steel.

Now he sits all alone, slipping into the past
in a car without engine or wheels
gazing far into friendly hills
where the passing years made wings for his
heels.

All signals are 'Go' as he steams away –
alongside the track are meadows in flower
ferociously happy he gives a toot
to the witch who lives in the water tower.

His mind is at one with the greening fields
which give him a welcoming smile
and Spring holds out a big 'Glad Hand'
which he grips for mile after mile.

So much a part of the old routine
he dissolves in the daily round
and the snow which is falling and chilling
the air
is May blossom falling around.

Jonty is riding the footplate again
like a chariot into heaven
adrenaline running, the train dead on time
a man of steel to the end of the line.

A man travels fastest who travels alone
but I wish he sold tickets.

A Fine Romance

It was breakfast time at the 'GRAND'
as Dolly made her way to the table,
smile fixed firmly in place –
her all-purpose greeting to the world.
A little over-generous with the lipstick
but that was Dolly.
A heavy glass vase stood centre table
proud with exotic orchids.

The smile became slightly brittle.
Birthday? No. Christmas? No.
So who was playing the fool
with a sixty year plump lady?

The flowers were real to her enquiring fingers,
flesh on flesh to Dolly's starving touch.
The exquisite feel of another hand,
young days lit by Spring.

Conditioned by long years of Agatha Christie
her big heart searched for a plot,
looking round for Cary Grant
she saw a cleaner. That was it!
Dumped there for convenience.
Silly cow, playing fast and loose with
heartache,

the yearning … never faced eyeball to eyeball.

Lonely as a wandering star she stared at the
morning,
remembering the wedding of yesterday,
the togetherness of laughing guests ..
with a longing so intense it was almost a
physical touch.

It WAS a physical touch – on the shoulder –
and a waitress mouthed one word
'Sorry'
and swept the flowers away.

Dolly, a permanent guest at the GRAND,
dredged up a smile.

It was what you did when you were on your
own.
It stood proxy for a life.

Big Numbers

Well, look who it is, now fancy that
have you come for a little chat?
You'll have to tell me who you are
my memory's gone – did I tell you that?

I'm like Aunt Jane, in nursing care
a stare from a chair and nobody there.
So many chairs … in here.

It's somebody's birthday
some silly old bat.
My memory's gone. Did I tell you that?

Look at these cards, see that one shine
there's a number there, or is it a cat.
I think it might be a number nine
so one thing's for sure, it can't be mine.
Another nine? I didn't see that.

My daughter came just yesterday
brought me a cake and a kiss on the cheek
I told her to take it and give the staff
'cos somebody's ninety nine this week.

Just look at these cards, now isn't that kind
to put them here where I can see
'cos somebody's ninety nine this week …
two such big numbers – glad it's not me.

Fatty in the Tea Shop

There's a gossipy tea shop in high street
all lipstick and scarlet nails
where voices are urgent yet blossom soft
and absent folk are put on the scales.

The bay window is crowded with flowers
dyed, dried and drawn into line.
Roses and ribbons and pretty pink chintz
ruched and rigid as wedding cake
an aroma of exotic teas
China, Darjeeling, Siam.

There's a fan of sweet peas on the counter
painting the air a soft scented pink
while proud in a cut-glass shiny vase
a perfect trumpet of lilies
all Summer contained in a perfect display.

Then! The oozing sweet goodies arrive
a foaming frenzy of thick fresh cream
a blanket of raw throbbing sugar
pumped up busty buns, lovely crusty crumpets.
Sticky tacky twists of pastry
intimate on the tongue as a lover's kiss.

And I, straining my ears for the gossip

and sipping my sugarless tea
hear a voice, straight from the Easter Island,
savage, pitiless, barbaric.

Forget it! Not a bite.
It'll turn to cellulite. Overnight.

Clara and George

It was just a tweed coat
one of the many in the crowded high street
but the man pranced proudly along in it
like he'd had it all its life.
The cheek of him.

Of course it was a good coat.
Stood out a mile from all the others
but when was he going to stop fiddling with it,
pulling the lapels out of shape.
Clara looked at the fellow.
He was a bland expression. No more.
No appreciation of clothes – or people. So
obvious.

The sort who would throw a good coat over
a chair
for people to lean on – and crease.
Decorate it. Pencils in the top pocket.
Rubbish in the side pockets
corduroy trousers beneath
down at heel shoes, scuffed.
Not casual, just scruffy.
That's how he would be if you could see him
out of the crowd.

She glared at him with a look that would strip
rhubarb.

She wanted to strip it off him
swipe his funny shaped head with it.
Tears formed as she bit her lip.
The skunk. The no-account walking rag-bag.
The tears were a flood now
as the coat went serenely down the high street
away from the 'Help the Aged' shop
where she had donated all George's clothes
only three short months ago.
HE could never be George.

'TAKES MORE THAN A COAT, M'LAD.'

She glared after the poncing prat.

Last Act

His days are very quiet now
and resound with unspoken words
'impromptu' visits are carefully arranged
around watching and feeding the birds.

Quiet smiles are set in place
in a ritual taboo
you talk of the weather and Mrs. Jones
and for once you can talk about you.

But do not gaze at the gentle man
whose eyes are too big for his head
for to fix on someone who isn't there
would pronounce him already dead.

He never scored much at getting his way
he smiled at your arguments
and went in silence throughout the years
for fear of giving offence.

He was better at 'being' than making his mark
absorbing all nature gave
loving the trees when the time was green
for the shape or the light or the shade.

Now the clock ticks on in the quiet room

where life is ebbing away
while we hide behind a screen of talk –
a barrage of nothing to say.

We have hidden from death since we knew it
was there
since we learned that to think is to be
rehearsing our part for the final play
when the out-going 'star' will be me.